What's My Style?

I love creating elaborate patterns packed with detail so I can do lots of intricate coloring. I try to use as many colors as possible. Then I layer on lots of fun details. Here are some more examples of my work.

My studio is filled with natural light, tons of coloring supplies, and lots of inspiration, all of which motivate me to create and color!

Where to Start

You might find putting color on a fresh page stressful. It's okay! Here are a few tricks I use to get the ink flowing.

Start with an easy decision. If a design has leaves, without a doubt, that's where I start. No matter how wacky and colorful everything else gets, I always color the leaves in my illustrations green. I have no reason for it; it's just how it is! Try to find something in the design to help ground you by making an easy color decision: leaves are green, the sky is blue, etc.

Get inspired. Take a good look at everything in the illustration. You chose to color it for a reason. One little piece that you love will jump out and say, "Color me! Use red, please!" Or maybe it will say blue, or pink, or green. Just relax—it will let you know.

Follow your instincts. What colors do you love? Are you a big fan of purple? Or maybe yellow is your favorite. If you love it, use it!

Just go for it. Close your eyes, pick up a color, point to a spot on the illustration, and start! Sometimes starting is the hardest part, but it's the fastest way to finish!

Helpful Hints

There is no right or wrong. All colors work together, so don't be scared to mix it up. The results can be surprising!

Try it. Test your chosen colors on scrap paper before you start coloring your design. You can also test blending techniques and how to use different shapes and patterns for detail work—you can see how different media will blend with or show up on top of your chosen colors. I even use the paper to clean my markers or pens if necessary.

Make a color chart. A color chart is like a test paper for every single color you have! It provides a more accurate way to choose colors than selecting them based on the color of the marker's cap. To make a color chart, color a swatch with each marker, colored pencil, gel pen, etc. Label each swatch with the name or number of the marker so you can easily find it later.

Do you like warm colors?

How about cool colors?

Maybe you like warm and cool colors together!

Keep going. Even if you think you've ruined a piece, work through it. I go through the same cycle with my coloring: I love a piece at the beginning, and by the halfway point I nearly always dislike it. Sometimes by the end I love it again, and sometimes I don't, and that's okay. It's important to remember that you're coloring for you— no one else. If you really don't like a piece at the end, stash it away and remember that you learned something. You know what not to do next time. My studio drawers are full of everything from duds to masterpieces!

Be patient. Let markers, gel pens, and paints dry thoroughly between each layer. There's nothing worse than smudging a cluster of freshly inked dots across the page with your hand. Just give them a minute to dry and then you can move on to the next layer.

Use caution. Juicy/inky markers can "spit" when you uncap them. Open them away from your art piece.

Work from light to dark. It's much easier to make something darker gradually than to lighten it.

Shade with gray. A mid-tone lavender-gray marker is perfect for adding shadows to your artwork, giving it depth and making it pop right off the page!

Try blending fluid. If you like working with alcohol-based markers, a refillable bottle of blending fluid or a blending pen is a great investment. Aside from enabling you to easily blend colors together, it can help clean up unwanted splatters or mistakes—it may not take some colors away completely, but it will certainly lighten them. I use it to clean the body of my markers as I'm constantly smudging them with inky fingers. When a marker is running out of ink, I find adding a few drops of blending fluid to the ink barrel will make it last a bit longer.

Layering and Blending

I love layering and blending colors. It's a great way to create shading and give your finished piece lots of depth and dimension. The trick is to work from the lightest color to the darkest and then go over everything again with the lightest shade to keep the color smooth and bring all the layers together.

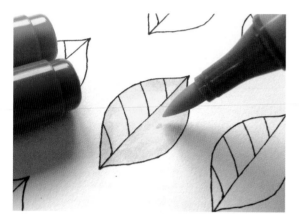

1 Apply a base layer with the lightest color.

2 Add the middle color, using it to create shading.

3 Smooth out the color by going over everything with the lightest color.

4 Add the darkest color, giving your shading even more depth. Use the middle color to go over the same area you colored in Step 2.

5 Go over everything with the lightest color as you did in Step 3.

Patterning and Details

Layering and blending will give your coloring depth and dimension. Adding patterning and details will really bring it to life. If you're not convinced, try adding a few details to one of your colored pieces with a white gel pen—that baby will make magic happen! Have fun adding all of the dots, doodles, and swirls you can imagine.

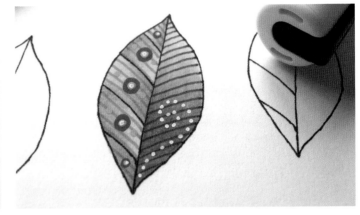

1 Once you've finished your coloring, blending, and layering, go back and add simple patterning like lines or dots. You can add your patterns in black or color. For this leaf, I used two different shades of green pen.

2 Now it's time to add some fun details using paint pens or gel pens. Here I used white, yellow, and more green.

This design really pops with lots of patterning and little details.

Coloring Supplies

I'm always asked about the mediums I use to color my illustrations. The answer would be really long if I listed every single thing, so here are a few of my favorites. Keep in mind that these are *my* favorites. When you color, you should use YOUR favorites!

Alcohol-based markers. I have many, and a variety of brands. My favorites have a brush nib—it's so versatile. A brush nib is perfect for tiny, tight corners, but is also able to cover a large, open space easily. I find I rarely get streaking, and if I do, it's usually because the ink is running low!

Fine-tip pens. Just like with markers, I have lots of different pens. I use them for my layers of detail work and for the itsy bitsy spots my markers can't get into.

Paint pens. These are wonderful! Because the ink is usually opaque, they stand out really well against a dark base color. I use extra fine point pens for their precision. Some paint pens are water based, so I can use a brush to blend the colors and create a cool watercolor effect.

Gel pens. I have a few, but I usually stick to white and neon colors that will stand out on top of dark base colors or other mediums.

Hello Angel #1297 Cat in the Safari Hat: markers, pens, paint pens

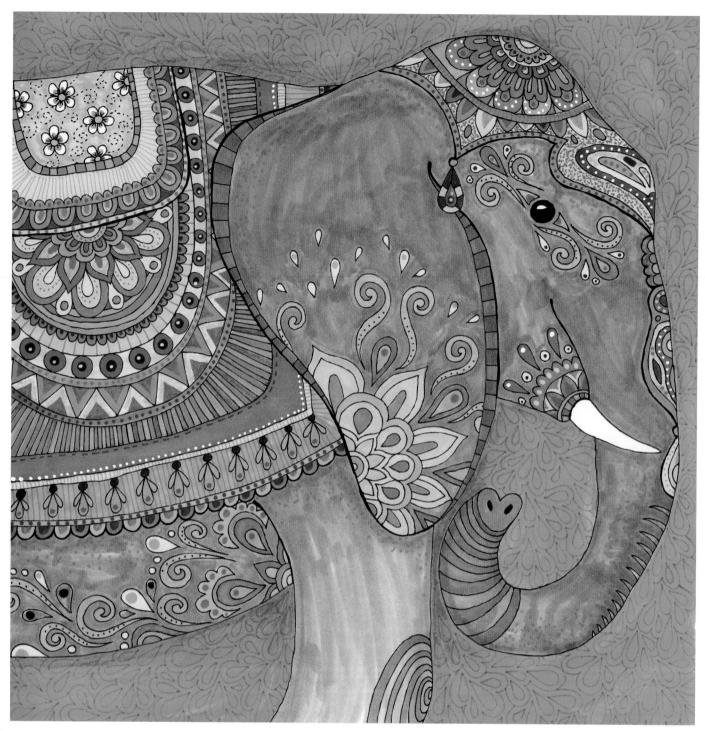

Hello Angel #1298 Portrait of a Pachyderm: markers, pens, paint pens

Hello Angel #1294 Trusty Compass: markers, pens, paint pens

Hello Angel #1300 Animal Medley: markers, pens, paint pens

Hello Angel #1301 Along for the Ride: markers, pens, paint pens, colored pencils

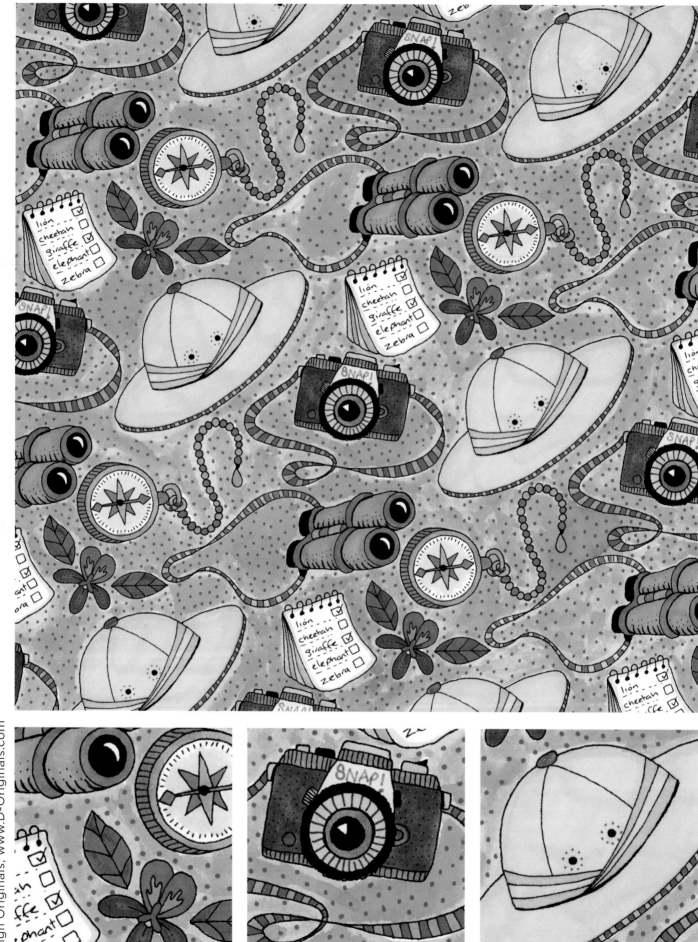

Hello Angel #1302 Goin' on Safari: markers, pens, paint pens

Hello Angel #1303 Happy Together: markers, pens, paint pens

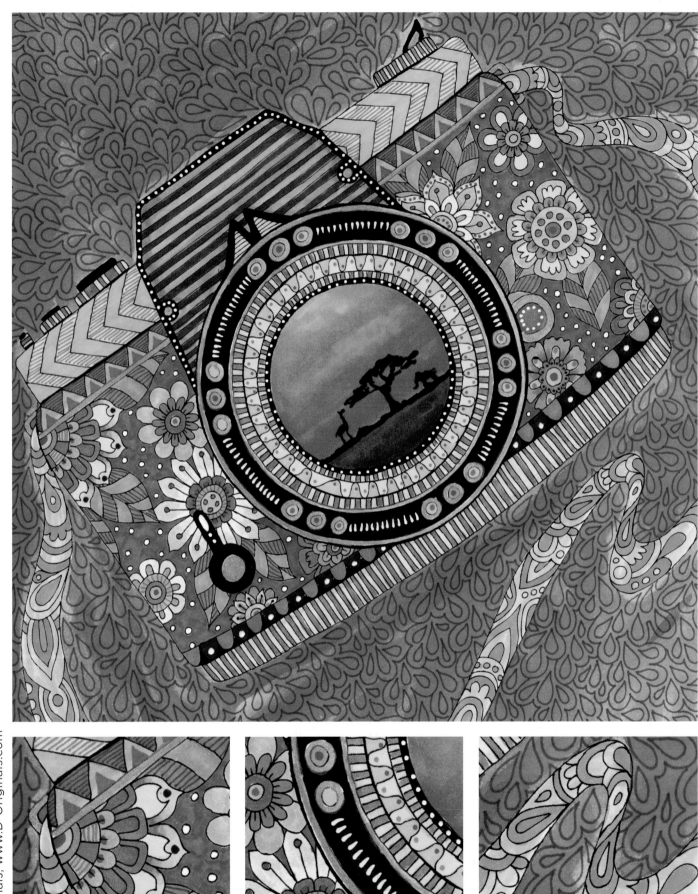

Hello Angel #1304 Safari Snapshot: markers, pens, paint pens

Travel made the best version of me.

—UNKNOWN

If there were one more thing I could do,
it would be to go on safari once again.

—Karen Blixen

Hello Angel #1290 Silhouette Parade

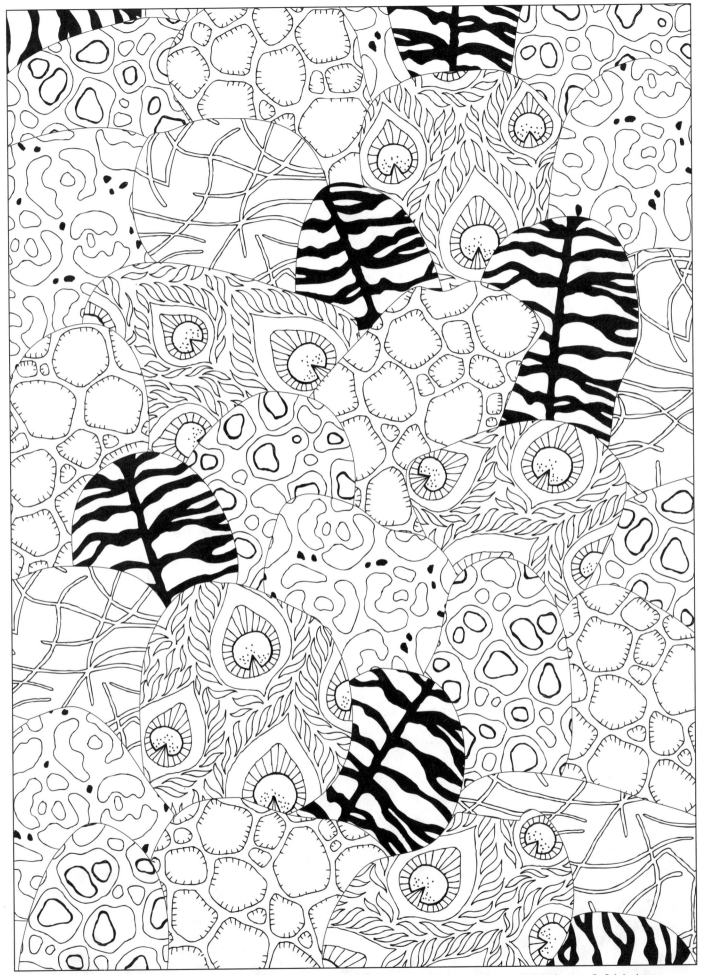

Pay attention to the
intricate patterns of your existence
that you take for granted.

—DOUG DILLON

_____

_____

_____

_____

_____

_____

_____

_____

_____

_____

_____

There is no Wi-Fi in the forest,
but I promise you will find
a better connection.

—UNKNOWN

Look deep into nature and you
will understand everything better.

—ALBERT EINSTEIN

_____
_____
_____
_____
_____
_____
_____
_____
_____

Life is either a daring adventure
or nothing.

—HELEN KELLER, *THE OPEN DOOR*

The traveler sees what he sees.
The tourist sees what he has come to see.

—G.K. CHESTERTON

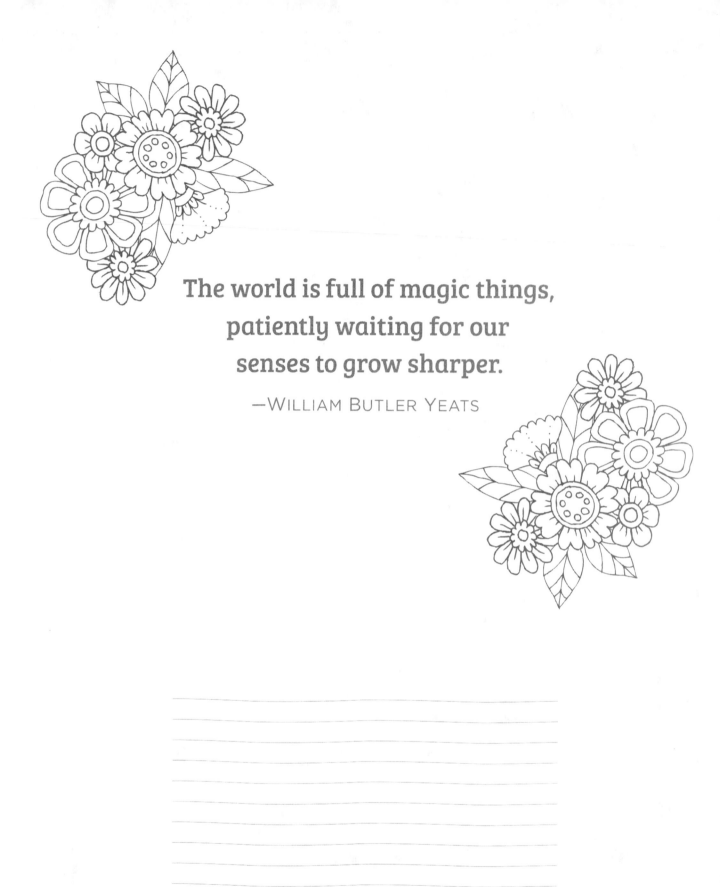

> The world is full of magic things,
> patiently waiting for our
> senses to grow sharper.

—WILLIAM BUTLER YEATS

Think like a makeup artist: use cool feature highlights against a warm, monochromatic mane, and you'll end up with a glam-rockin' safari lion!

Everything in Africa bites,
but the safari bug is worst of all.

—BRIAN JACKMAN

Hello Angel #1297 Cat in the Safari Hat

Elephants have thick hides, which you can show
by laying down some heavy marker.

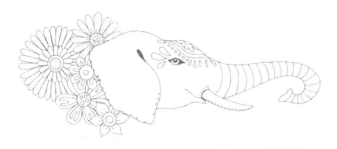

Blessed are the curious,
for they shall have adventures.

—UNKNOWN

Hello Angel #1298 Portrait of a Pachyderm

Who needs camouflage when you're queen of the jungle?
Use split complementary colors, like green and yellow,
to give your big cat an intense gaze.

A truly strong person does not need
the approval of others any more than a
lion needs the approval of sheep.

—VERNON HOWARD

_____
_____
_____
_____
_____
_____
_____
_____

Hello Angel #1299 Up Close

When faced with a complex design, don't overwhelm yourself: stick with a basic complementary palette, like warm brown eyes for cool faces and cool blue eyes for warm faces.

We all have a responsibility
to protect endangered species,
both for their sake
and for the sake of our
own future generations.

—LORETTA LYNCH

Hello Angel #1300 Animal Medley

Like parent, like child! Make a statement
with one tail, and then emphasize it by
replicating your color pattern in the other tail.

The earth is what we all have in common.

—WENDELL BERRY

Hello Angel #1301 Along for the Ride

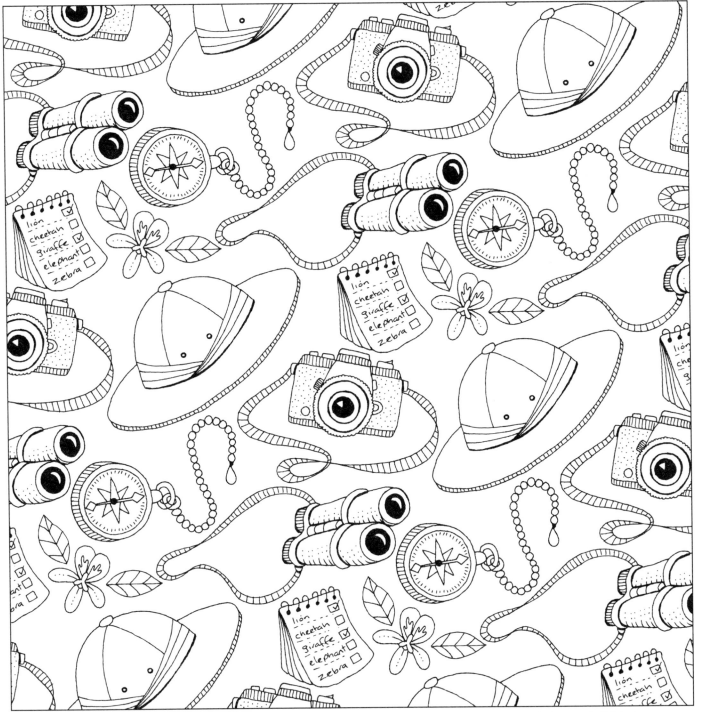

Bright objects really pop out from a darker, monochromatic background.

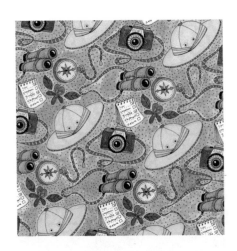

Holiday: A period of activity
so intense that it can only be undertaken
three or four weeks in the year.

—MILES KINGTON

Hello Angel #1302 Goin' on Safari

Visually highlight the natural harmony between these two different species by subtly replicating colors in each.

I could travel the world
and the ocean blue but I'll never be
home until I'm with you.

—Unknown

_____

_____

_____

_____

_____

_____

_____

_____

Hello Angel #1303 Happy Together

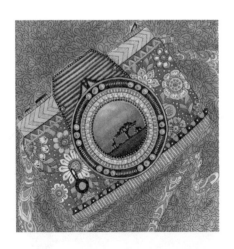

A flat background pumped full of electric color
turns any ordinary coloring into a showstopper.

A good snapshot keeps
a moment from running away.

—EUDORA WELTY

Hello Angel #1304 Safari Snapshot

In Wildness is the preservation of the world.

—HENRY DAVID THOREAU, "WALKING"

I haven't been everywhere,
but it's on my list.

—Susan Sontag

Curiosity is one of the
great secrets of happiness.

—Bryant McGill

Live in the sunshine,
swim the sea,
drink the wild air.

—Ralph Waldo Emerson,
"Merlin's Song"

Let's make today an
adventure kind of day.

—Unknown

The love for all living creatures
is the most noble attribute of man.

—CHARLES DARWIN

_____
_____
_____
_____
_____
_____
_____
_____
_____
_____

I think I could turn and live with animals,
they are so placid and self-contain'd,
I stand and look at them long and long.

—WALT WHITMAN, "SONG OF MYSELF"

_____
_____
_____
_____
_____
_____
_____
_____
_____

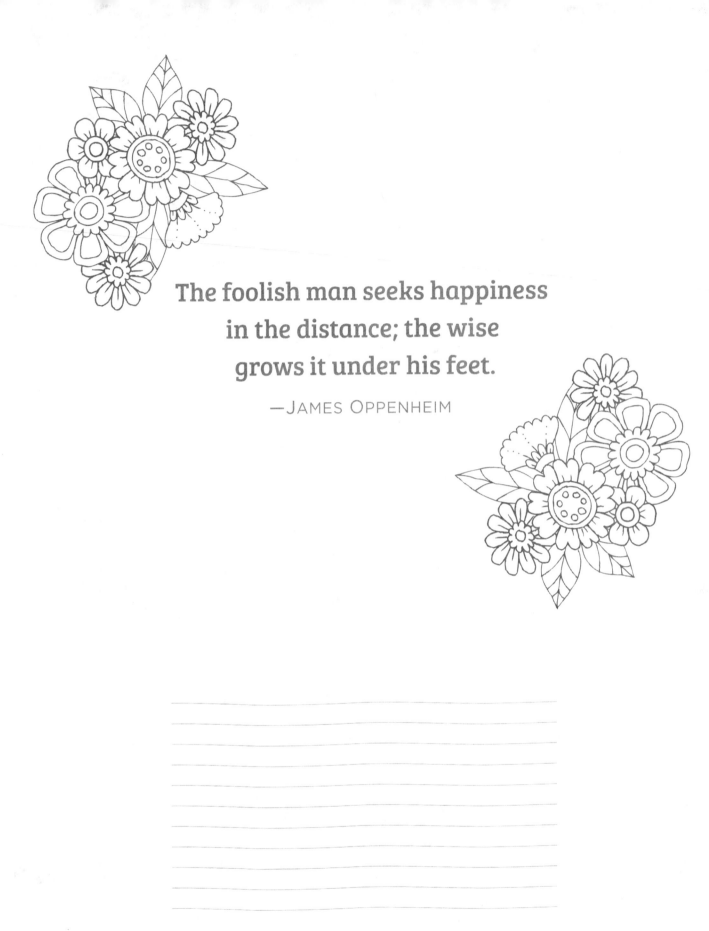

The foolish man seeks happiness
in the distance; the wise
grows it under his feet.

—JAMES OPPENHEIM

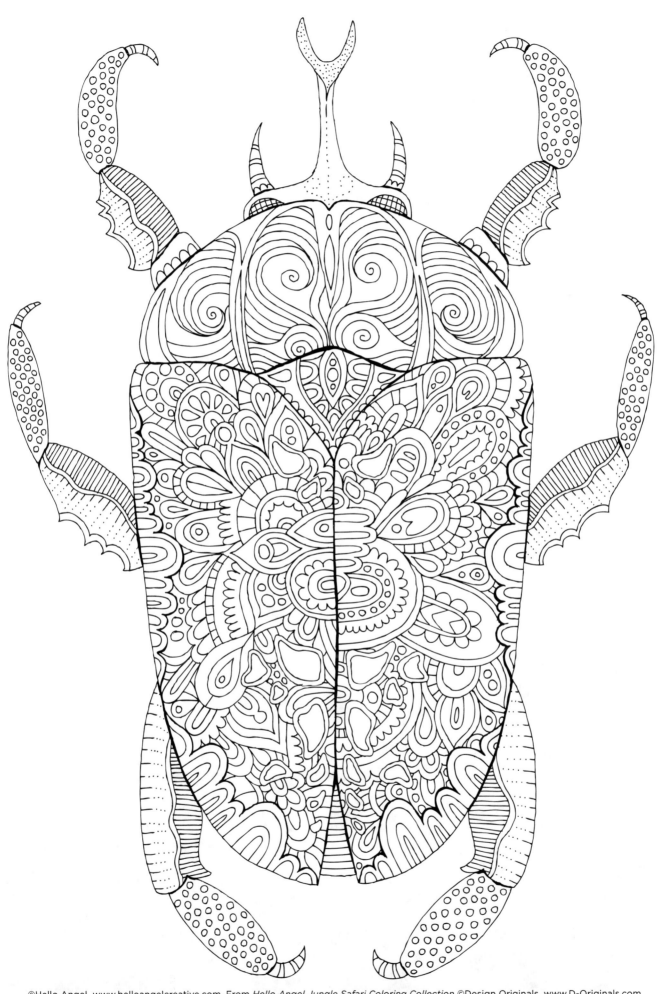

Live, travel, adventure,
bless and don't be sorry.

—JACK KEROUAC, *DESOLATION ANGELS*

Civilization no longer needs to open up wilderness; it needs wilderness to help open up the still largely unexplored human mind.

—DAVID RAINS WALLACE

We must take adventures in order
to know where we truly belong.

—UNKNOWN

_____
_____
_____
_____
_____
_____
_____
_____
_____
_____

Roses red and violets blew,
And all the sweetest flowres
that in the forest grew.

—EDMUND SPENSER, *FAERIE QUEENE*

Don't look back.
You're not going that way.

—UNKNOWN

I'm not beautiful like you.
I'm beautiful like me.

—JOYDROP, "BEAUTIFUL"

_____
_____
_____
_____
_____
_____
_____
_____
_____

Hello Angel #1318 Crowned Beauty

Learn to see, and then you'll know that there is no end to the new worlds of our vision.

—CARLOS CASTANEDA

I can't think of anything that excites a greater sense of childlike wonder than to be in a country where you are ignorant of almost everything.

—BILL BRYSON, *NEITHER HERE NOR THERE*

_____

_____

_____

_____

_____

_____

_____

_____

_____

_____

Hello Angel #1320 At Home in the Trees